TALES OF HEAVEN AND EARTH

Françoise Lebrun studied Literature and Politics at university.
She then became an actress and a collector of stories.
Several of her collections of stories have been published.

Cover design by Peter Bennett

ISBN: 1 85103 251 7
© Editions Gallimard, 1994
Managing editor: Jacqueline Vallon
Adviser for UK edition: Rev. David Jarmy
English text © 1996 by Moonlight Publishing Ltd
First published in the United Kingdom 1996
by Moonlight Publishing Ltd, 36 Stratford Road, London W8
Printed in Italy by Editoriale Zanardi

THE MAGIC
OF
CHRISTMAS

by Françoise Lebrun

Illustrated by Andrée Bienfait,
Dorothée Duntze, Jean-Marie
Poissenot, Valérie Stetten,
Dominique Thibault, Nicolas Wintz
Cover by François Place

Translated by Sarah Matthews

Moonlight Publishing

For my parents,
who taught me about festivals,
gave me a taste for dreams
and encouraged my sense of adventure.

The Christ child is born, but Mary is not strong enough to swaddle him.

The miracle of the spider

These stories come from the apocryphal New Testament, early non-Biblical Christian books.

Caesar Augustus, Emperor of Rome, had commanded a census of the entire Roman Empire. Every single person had to have their names recorded, returning to the town where they were born to register. Joseph and Mary travelled from Nazareth to Bethlehem, which is the city of King David, from whom Joseph was descended.

The sun was sinking over Bethlehem. For weeks, people had been cramming into the little town, upsetting its peaceful routine. Every kind of person was there, from the richest to the poorest. Mary and Joseph were among the last to arrive, travelling slowly because Mary was pregnant. Exhausted, they pushed their way through the crowds, looking for somewhere to stay. Joseph knocked at one inn door after another, without success. He came to the very last inn of all, and rapped on the door.

"Go and see who it is," said the innkeeper to one of his

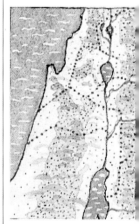

Palestine, 1st century AD.

The only person who agrees to help Mary has no arms!

servants, "but don't let them in unless they have gold or silver."

"I have neither gold nor silver," replied Joseph, "but all we are asking for is a handful of hay, and a roof over our heads to shelter us from the bitter night."

"Away with you! We don't house beggars here!" said the innkeeper.

But the innkeeper had a kind and gentle son, who grew angry with his father. "Your greed will be your downfall, father. Give these poor people shelter, even if it's only in the stable with the donkey." Joseph and Mary were shown to the stable, where an ox and an ass were resting in the gloom. They stretched out next to the animals, and Joseph was soon fast asleep. It wasn't long before Mary woke him: "Joseph, Joseph, wake up, the baby is coming!" She had hardly finished speaking when Jesus was born. Joseph gathered some hay together to make him a bed. Mary lay back with her naked baby cradled in her arms. "Oh, Joseph," she said, weak with tiredness, "I'm not going to be able to wrap the baby in his swaddling clothes all by myself. Go to the inn, and get one of the girls to

The stories are not always the same. There are no shepherds and no crib in Matthew's account, while Luke (above) doesn't mention the three kings.

come and help me."
Joseph ran to the inn and begged for help.

"Go and ask somewhere else," grumbled the innkeeper. "My daughters are asleep and the servants are busy."

"What about that young girl sitting over by the fire, couldn't she come?" asked Joseph.

"Hear that, Bertha?" sneered the innkeeper. "Go along with him then."

Without saying a word, Bertha followed Joseph to the stable. She reached out towards Mary, who saw that, where Bertha's arms and hands should have been, she had nothing but empty sleeves and two short stumps.

"Oh, you poor girl," said Mary. "How hard things must be for you. But look, you haven't come for nothing."

Mary held out the baby Jesus and laid him on the girl's knee. Immediately, Bertha found she had arms and hands with which to wrap the child in his swaddling clothes as he smiled up at her. Above, in the night sky, angels flew silently on silver wings, singing, "Glory, glory, glory to the Lord God of hosts! Heaven and earth are full of His glory."

It was not long after this that King Herod heard the disturbing news that a new king had been born.

It is only in the apocryphal gospels that there appear stories about the ox and the ass, about Bertha (sometimes called Anastasia) or about talking animals.

Below, a nativity scene according to an 18th century icon.

The apocryphal gospels (from a Greek word which means hidden) do not form part of the official writings of the Church.

Afraid for his throne, he sent out the command that all babies less than two years old should be killed. Joseph and Mary fled to Egypt with their baby son. But the baby was small, Mary was still weak, and they could not go fast. The soldiers were close behind them. Joseph saw a shallow cave where they could hide. The small family squeezed in. "Move further back," said Joseph urgently. "The soldiers will see us here."

"But if I do," replied Mary, "I'll squash the spider on the wall behind me."

"Quick, take my place," said the spider. Scuttling to the mouth of the cave, she quickly spun a magnificent web right across it.

Soon, the soldiers came past. They were going to search the cave, but they saw the spider's web. "They can't be here," said the sergeant. "There's a web right across the entrance and it hasn't been disturbed." And the soldiers moved on.

That is why, if you look at spiders' webs in the early morning, you'll see them scattered with Mary's tears, as she wept in gratitude over the tiny animal which had saved her baby son.

The Return from Egypt according to a fresco from Lambach Abbey in Austria.

In Islam, the prophet Muhammad has a similar adventure. While travelling to Madinah, pursued by enemies, he hides in a cave across which a spider has spun a huge web, so saving the prophet and the religion of Islam.

On New Year's Eve, some stones in Brittany come to life, but beware!

The tale of the flying stones

From a 19th century legend from Brittany, France.

Korrigan is a Breton word meaning wicked goblin.

Above, Brittany is marked in red.

Plouhinec is a small village in Brittany, close to the sea. All around it lie dark pine forests and sandy wastes of heathlands stretching down to the sea. Just outside the village, korrigans had put up two rows of tall stones. It would have looked like an avenue, if it had been going anywhere.

Not far away, down by the riverside, there once lived a man called Marzin. Marzin was rich and proud. He had refused to allow his sister Rozen to marry a number of the local young men, including a young man called Bernez, who

Standing stones, or menhir, were put up in megalithic times, some 4 to 6 thousand years ago. It is assumed that they were used for religious rituals. At Stonehenge, in England, the stones are arranged in such a way that, at dawn on Midsummer's Day, the rays of the sun strike directly onto one of the stones.

9

was a good Christian and a steady worker, but who had no fortune except his own good nature. Bernez had known Rozen ever since they were children, and they had always loved each other, so, despite Marzin's refusal, Bernez still hoped that somehow they could be married.

It was Christmas. A terrible storm had meant that it was impossible to get to church, so everyone on the farm had gathered together in the warmth of the house, joined by several young men from the neighbourhood, including Bernez. Just as they were all sitting down to supper, the door was flung open and an old man appeared. He was a local beggar, ragged and dirty. He never went to church, and it was said he could do black magic, shrivelling the crops and making strange potions. It was even said he might be a werewolf. But still, he was poor, and it was bitterly cold, so the farmer told him to warm himself at the fire and gave him something to eat.

When the magician had finished his meal, he asked for somewhere to sleep, and was shown to the stable. An old donkey and a sickly ox were snuggled down in the straw. The magician lay down between them to keep warm, and was soon drifting into sleep when he heard the church bells ring out. It was midnight. At that moment, the old donkey shook his ears and turned towards the ox: "Well, old friend,

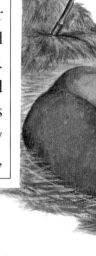

how have you been since last Christmas, when last we spoke together?"

Instead of answering, the ox looked sideways at the figure of the beggar huddled in the straw. "It's all very well, he grumbled, "God giving us the power of speech on Christmas Eve as thanks for being there when Jesus was born, if we've only got this old heap of rags to hear us."

"I've got more reason to complain than you have," said the donkey. "After all, my ancestor carried the Saviour on his back when he entered Jerusalem. That's why we all bear the cross marked on our backs. Anyway, what does it matter? Can't you see he's asleep?"

"All his magic isn't doing him much good," replied the ox. "He's losing his eternal soul for rags and scraps, and the Devil hasn't even told about the riches he could have a few days from now."

"What riches are those?" asked the donkey.

"What," said the ox, "don't you know that, every hundred years, the stones of Plouhinec go down to the river to bathe, and, during that time, the treasure they sit on lies open to the sky?"

"Oh, yes, I remember now," said the donkey. "But the stones fly back to their places so quickly that you will be crushed to death unless you have a sprig of vervain and

Christians celebrate the entry into Jerusalem on Palm Sunday. This 12th century picture is from Saint Mark's in Venice.

a five-leafed clover to protect you."

"What's more," said the ox, "the treasure will crumble into dust unless you give the stones a Christian soul in return; the Demon will not release his treasure without the death of a Christian."

The beggar had been listening closely to the conversation.

"Don't you worry, dear animals," he said to himself, "I won't be losing my soul for mere scraps any more."

Early next morning, the magician rose with the dawn and walked far off into the countryside to search for vervain and for a five-leafed clover. It took him many days, and it was only on New Year's Eve that he returned to Plouhinec. As he was walking across the heath, he saw Bernez working with his hammer and chisel, carving something into the largest of the stones.

"Are you trying to dig a house out of the stone?" asked the beggar with a laugh.

"No," replied Bernez, "but as I am out of work at the moment, I thought I would carve a cross into one of these stones, to please God."

"Is there something you want from Him, then?"

"All Christians want God to grant them salvation," replied the young man.

"Haven't you got anything else to ask him for then,

Clover usually only has three leaves. Occasionally you can find four, five, six or even seven-leafed clovers, but they are extremely rare. Because of their rarity, they were thought to bring good luck.

Vervain is a common European herbaceous plant, Verbena officinalis which used to be valued for its medicinal and magical properties. It was used to cure all sorts of ills and, if picked on Midsummer's Day or on Christmas Day, could give the user the power to find treasure, or to become invisible.

12

anything to do with Rozen?" asked the magician quietly.

"Ah, you know about that, do you?" said Bernez sadly. "Yes, Marzin wants a brother-in law richer than I could ever be."

"What if I helped you get more riches than Marzin could ever dream of?" asked the magician.

"You?"

"Me!"

"What would you want from me in return?"

"Only that you remember me in your prayers."

"Done!" Bernez exclaimed enthusiastically. "Just tell me what I have to do. I'll risk thirty thousand deaths to marry Rozen!"

The beggar told Bernez all about the stones going down to the river to bathe, and the treasure being uncovered. He said nothing, though, about the need for magic herbs for protection, or the death of a Christian soul. Bernez thought that all you needed to get the treasure was speed and courage.

"Just let me finish carving this cross, and I'll be with you."

Just before midnight, Bernez joined the magician at the spot where they had agreed to meet. The magician had three large sacks, one in each hand, and a third tied round his neck. As midnight arrived, the two men heard a strange

At the time the story is set, there was no paper money – the greatest riches would have been in gold coins like the one below, which dates from 1704.

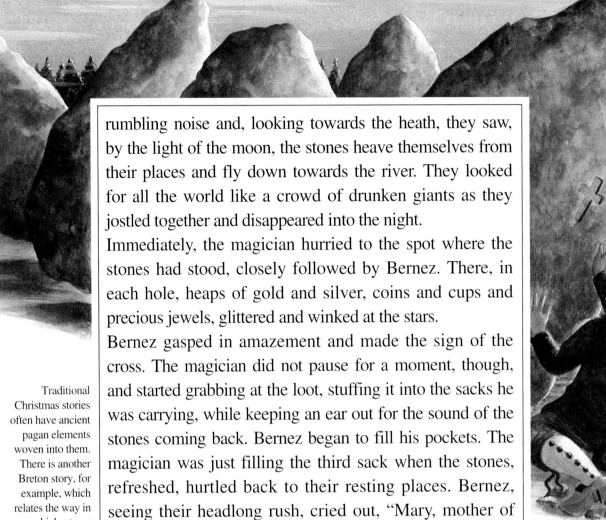

rumbling noise and, looking towards the heath, they saw, by the light of the moon, the stones heave themselves from their places and fly down towards the river. They looked for all the world like a crowd of drunken giants as they jostled together and disappeared into the night.

Immediately, the magician hurried to the spot where the stones had stood, closely followed by Bernez. There, in each hole, heaps of gold and silver, coins and cups and precious jewels, glittered and winked at the stars.

Bernez gasped in amazement and made the sign of the cross. The magician did not pause for a moment, though, and started grabbing at the loot, stuffing it into the sacks he was carrying, while keeping an ear out for the sound of the stones coming back. Bernez began to fill his pockets. The magician was just filling the third sack when the stones, refreshed, hurtled back to their resting places. Bernez, seeing their headlong rush, cried out, "Mary, mother of God, protect us, we are lost!"

"Not me," said the magician, holding up the vervain and the five-leafed clover. "But they need the death of a Christian to let me keep the riches. Forget Rozen, and prepare to die!"

While he was speaking, the army of stones arrived. The magician held up his magic herbs and the stones swerved

Traditional Christmas stories often have ancient pagan elements woven into them. There is another Breton story, for example, which relates the way in which, at one special moment during Midnight Mass, all creatures ever created, living and dead, appear for a moment: fairies, demons, werewolves, souls in Purgatory, saints, angels...

round him, turning to the left and to the right and rounding on Bernez. The young man fell to his knees. He was about to shut his eyes in terror when he saw the largest stone, which was at the head of the grim army, stop dead in front of him, as if to shield him.

Bernez, astonished, looked up at the stone, and realised that it was the very one in which he had earlier carved the sign of the cross. It was now a baptised stone and could not harm a Christian. It stayed still, shielding the young man, until all its companions had settled back in their places, then it took off for its own position. As it flew along, it came upon the magician, who was weighed down by his sacks of treasure. Seeing the stone flying towards him, the magician held out his magic herbs, but the stone was now Christian, and no longer prey to the Devil's magic. Without swerving, it flew to its resting place, knocking the magician to one side and crushing him like an insect.

Bernez had all the treasure he had collected himself, and the three sackfuls that the magician had collected. Now he was rich enough to marry Rozen and to have as many bonny children as a wren has chicks in her nest.

In Brittany, the wren symbolises the death of the old year and the hope for a new life. Often the priest would release a wren in the church on Christmas Day.

"Come with us, Babushka!" said the three kings, but she hesitated.

Babushka

This story comes
from Russia.

Sometimes, on Christmas night, when the snow lies deep
on the ground, covering fields and hedgerows in a crisp,
glittering blanket, you can see a little old woman going
slowly from village to village. Her face is a mass of
wrinkles, she leans on a stick to help her battle through the
wind and snow, in her hand she carries a chunk of thick
black bread, while on her back hangs a sack stuffed with
strange shapes.

She has been walking like this since one winter's evening
long, long ago.

In Russian
stories, babushka
is the typical
figure of an old
peasant woman.

In northern
Russia, peasant
cottages were
built of pine
wood. They had a
big central stove.

ARCTIC OCEAN

RUSSIA

MIDDLE
EAST   CHINA

Russia today

16

She had been sitting in her cottage, snug and warm next to the fire, when she heard knocking at the door. "Someone must be lost in the snow," she said to herself, and hurried across to let them in. Outside, she was astonished to see three tall men, their beards hung about with icicles, their faces serious, their eyes shining in the dark night. "Grandmother, Babushka," said one of the men, "We have come from far away, and we wanted to let you know our news before we travel on. A great prince has been born tonight, a prince who will save the world. We don't know quite where he is, but we are following a star which will guide us. Would you like to come too?" Babushka was taken by surprise. She didn't know what to say. It was so cold, she was so old, the snow was so thick... She tried to keep them there until morning, saying that they should warm themselves and have something to eat, so that she could, in her own words, "mull it over." But nothing could keep the men

The three kings were wise men from the East who went to Bethlehem to pay homage to the baby Jesus. The gospels do not say that they were kings, nor how many of them there were. Below, a stained glass window from Köln in Germany.

In the 11th century, the kings were given names, Caspar, Balthazar and Melchior. They gradually acquired other characteristics: Caspar was young, Melchior middle-aged, Balthazar old. In the 15th century, Balthazar was said to come from Africa, Melchior from the Far East, Caspar from Europe.

She has been searching for the Christ child ever since.

there. "We are in too much of a hurry, Babushka," they said, and disappeared into the night. After they had gone, Babushka could not settle. "I never asked them how they had heard the news, or where they thought they would find the little prince. I'll go after them first thing in the morning and catch them up. And I'll take some presents for the baby." She spent the rest of the night making little presents, toys and pretty, coloured nuts.

At dawn, she set off. Every time she met someone, she asked after the little prince, but no-one knew where he was. Some answered kindly, some made fun of her. But still she went on. She knew the prince was somewhere.

Every Christmas night, while everyone is asleep, she creeps into the houses, and gazes down on the sleeping children. "What if this is the little prince?" she murmurs to herself, a tear trickling down her wrinkled cheeks, and puts a present down on the bed for the sleeping child. Before setting off again, she takes a bite from her chunk of black bread. Sometimes a few crumbs can be found scattered in the shoes of the child who was, for that night, the little prince...

In Italy, another old lady, la Befana, has a similar experience. She too did not go with the three kings when they asked her and has been seeking the baby Jesus ever since. According to some versions, Saint Nicholas took her for a witch. She brings presents to children on the feast of the Epiphany, the 6th of January.

The star of Bethlehem is linked to astrological beliefs of the time. It is often said that strange cosmic phenomena accompany the birth of great leaders and wise men, such as the Buddha.

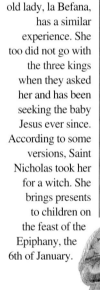

In the forest of Göinge, there lived a robber and his family.

This story is adapted from a 19th century story by the Swedish author, Selma Lagerlöf.

The Christmas rose

The thief who lived in a cave in the hills in Göinge forest was an outlaw. Because of his wickedness, he could find no shelter in town or village, on pain of death. He scratched a living by robbing any travellers unwary enough to set foot in his corner of the forest. Meanwhile his wife and their five children went out begging, dressed in skins, with shoes made of bark, and each carrying a sack as big as themselves. No-one dared refuse the beggar-woman, for they knew full well that she would not hesitate to set fire to their houses or their farms if she

This story takes place in southern Sweden (marked in red on the map opposite). Christianity was introduced into Sweden around 830. At that time southern Sweden was a province of Denmark.

19

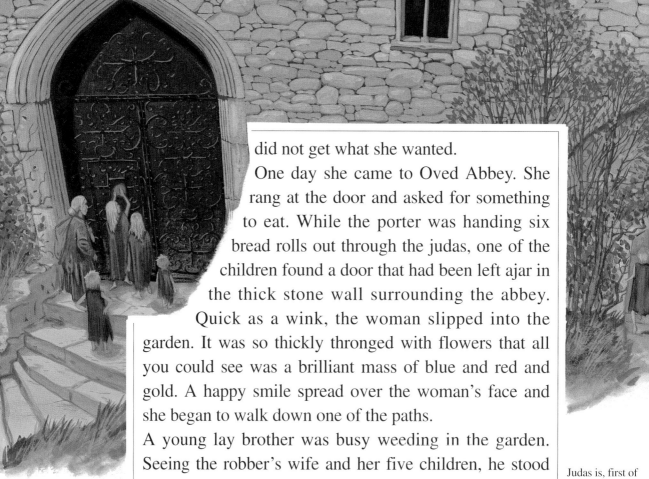

did not get what she wanted.

One day she came to Oved Abbey. She rang at the door and asked for something to eat. While the porter was handing six bread rolls out through the judas, one of the children found a door that had been left ajar in the thick stone wall surrounding the abbey.

Quick as a wink, the woman slipped into the garden. It was so thickly thronged with flowers that all you could see was a brilliant mass of blue and red and gold. A happy smile spread over the woman's face and she began to walk down one of the paths.

A young lay brother was busy weeding in the garden. Seeing the robber's wife and her five children, he stood in front of them and tried to shoo them out. But she just kept on going, gazing around her. The lay brother thought she had not understood what he wanted, and took her by the arm to take her back to the gate. The beggar-woman glared at him so fiercely that he let her go and stepped away from her. Up until then she had been hunched over, her sack on her back. Now she drew herself up to her full height. "I am the robber's wife," she declared. "Touch me at your peril." The young lay brother still asked her to leave, but she took no notice.

A lay brother is a man who is not a priest, but who lives and works in a monastery.

Judas is, first of all, the name of the disciple who betrayed Jesus and delivered him to his enemies. It is also the name given to the small opening in a door or wall which allows someone to look out while not being seen.

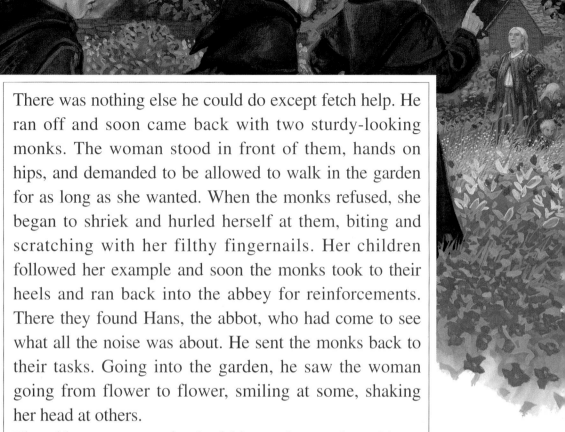

The word abbot comes from the Latin word abbas, which means father. The abbot was thought of as the father of the monks. The Benedictine order, founded by Saint Benedict, elected the abbot for life.

There was nothing else he could do except fetch help. He ran off and soon came back with two sturdy-looking monks. The woman stood in front of them, hands on hips, and demanded to be allowed to walk in the garden for as long as she wanted. When the monks refused, she began to shriek and hurled herself at them, biting and scratching with her filthy fingernails. Her children followed her example and soon the monks took to their heels and ran back into the abbey for reinforcements. There they found Hans, the abbot, who had come to see what all the noise was about. He sent the monks back to their tasks. Going into the garden, he saw the woman going from flower to flower, smiling at some, shaking her head at others.

The abbot was very fond of his garden, and could not help but admire this woman, who had fought off three men. He walked up to her and asked her politely whether she liked the garden. The woman turned round quickly, but, seeing the abbot's white hair and his stooped figure, she replied quietly, "At first I thought I had never seen a more beautiful garden, but now I see it's not as lovely as another garden I know."

Hans coloured slightly, while the lay brother tried to put the woman in her place, "How can you say that, you who

live in the wild woods! Everyone knows that there's no more beautiful garden in the whole region that the garden of abbot Hans!"

"That may be true, but you monks ought to know that every Christmas Eve the forest of Göinge is transformed into a paradise in honour of the hour our Saviour was born. If you were allowed to see it, you would tear up the flowers here, and throw them away as weeds and tares."

The abbot signalled to the lay brother to keep quiet. Ever since his childhood he had heard tell of the way in which, on Christmas Eve, the forest became a riot of colour. But he had never been able to witness this miracle. He begged the robber's wife to let him come to their cave on Christmas Eve. He promised not to betray them, and to do everything in his power to help them. Eventually, the woman agreed.

Now, it happened that some time later Absalom, Archbishop of Lund came to Oved and stayed at the abbey overnight. While Hans was showing the Archbishop his garden, his meeting with the robber's wife came back to mind. He told the Archbishop about the robber who had lived up in the hills all these years,

Tare is a weed which infests wheat crops. If eaten, it can make people feel dizzy and drunk. In the New Testament, 'separating the wheat from the tares' means separating the good from the wicked.

...the old abbot of Oved abbey decided to visit them.

In religious terms, the word absolution means the forgiveness of sins by the priest after confession. In law, it means the repeal of all punishments to which an offender has been condemned. In this way, the robber would be forgiven his sins and freed from the punishment of men.

and he asked the Archbishop for a letter of absolution so that the robber could begin to live an honest life again. "Otherwise," the abbot went on, "his children will grow up to be even more dangerous than he is, and we'll have a whole robber band up in the hills." The Archbishop replied that they could not allow such villains to live with honest folk. Hans then told him the tale of the Christmas miracle, and ended by saying, "If these robbers are allowed to see the splendour of God then surely they should be allowed the mercy of men." The Archbishop did not know what to say. He smiled at the Abbot and replied, "I'll tell you what. You bring me a flower from the Christmas garden in Göinge forest, and I'll give you a letter of absolution for the robber."

The following Christmas, Hans set off for Göinge forest, taking the lay brother with him. One of the robber's children ran ahead, showing them the way. The abbot was delighted, but the lay brother was far from happy. The further they went, the more uneasy he became, and he begged the abbot to turn back. The abbot would have none of it, and they pressed on, the way getting wilder and wilder, the snow deeper, the narrow paths winding ever up the hillside, over bogs and rocks and fallen trees. The sun was setting as the child led them into a clearing

Absalom, the Archbishop of Lund, really existed. Educated in Paris, he founded Copenhagen around 1167. The Swedish church was dependent on the Arbishropric of Lund, and so it was to the highest figure in the Scandinavian church that the abbot had turned to seek absolution for the robber.

surrounded by tall pines swaying and sighing in the wind. At the edge of the clearing stood a great rock, and behind it a door of roughly cut planks. Hans realised that they had arrived. Inside the cave, the robber's wife was

sitting beside a crackling log fire. The robber was asleep on a bed made of twigs and moss. "Come in," said his wife without getting up. "Sit down by the fire, father abbot, and eat, if you've brought food with you. Then you can sleep. I'll wake you when it's time."

Hans got out the provisions he had brought, but he was so tired he could hardly bring himself to eat and soon fell into a deep sleep. The lay brother did not dare go to sleep. He felt it was his duty to stand guard over the abbot, but soon tiredness overcame him, and he too went to sleep. When he awoke, he saw the abbot talking to the woman over by the fire. The robber was sitting to one side, his face brooding and sad. Suddenly, the woman got

At midnight, they saw an amazing sight.

up. "Listen!" she said, "Christmas bells!"

Everyone piled out of the cave into the black and bitter night. Without warning, a bright light flared up over the forest, then died away again, making the darkness even blacker than before. Then the light flared up again, and again, and gradually the sky was filled with the brilliant colours of the Northern Lights. The snow disappeared and grass grew fresh and green. The abbot's eyes filled with tears. Sounds began to fill the forest: the rippling waters of streams, the rustling of leaves unfolding like bright butterflies' wings on all the trees, birdcalls from birds with brilliant feathers which flashed between the trees. As light played over the forest, a warm breeze sprang up, carrying on it seeds which landed and germinated where they fell, springing up in a host of pretty flowers. The birds began to build nests. In the distance, shepherds called to their cows, and sheep-bells clanged far away. Fruit ripened on the trees. The abbot stooped to pick a flower from a strawberry plant. As he stood up, the fruit swelled and ripened. A vixen brought out her cubs to play on the soft grass.

The robber's children squealed with delight, filling their mouths with berries. One played with a jackdaw, while another had a viper coiled around its arm. The

This garden of Eden in the forest recalls the lines from the Bible: The wolf also shall dwell with the lamb, and the leopard shall lie down with the kid, and the calf and young lion and the fatling together... and the sucking child shall play on the hole of the asp... for the earth shall be full of the knowledge of the Lord, as the waters cover the sea. (Isaiah 11, verses 6-9.)

robber gathered blackberries, watched by a solemn bear. From a beehive hanging from an oak tree honey overflowed and dripped to the ground. Hans remembered the promise he had made to Archbishop Absalom, but he hesitated to pick a flower, as each one which appeared was more beautiful than the one before, and he wanted to take the Archbishop the most beautiful one of all.

Suddenly, an enormous calm settled over the forest, birds fell silent, flowers ceased to grow. A low murmur began to swell through the trees, and the abbot glimpsed radiant forms between the branches. He fell to his knees, overwhelmed with happiness. Never had he thought to taste the joys of heaven in this life, and to hear angels sing hymns to the glory of the newborn Christ.

Beside him, the lay brother stood, tense and anxious. He was certain that this vision, revealed to robbers and criminals, must come from the Devil. Just then, a dove landed on his shoulder and rubbed its soft face against his cheek. Roughly, he knocked it off, crying out, "Return to

Below, a stained glass window showing a singing angel (Evreux, 14th century).

According to the Bible, angels are spiritual intermediaries between people and God. They are divided into three groups: cherubim, seraphim and thrones form the first group; dominions, virtues and powers, the second; archangels and angels, the third and last group.

But the young  *monk broke the spell.*

Hell, from whence you came!"
Immediately, the heavenly singing stopped,
darkness descended like a black shroud
over the forest, the plants shrivelled, the animals
fled, leaves fell from the trees and the streams became
silent. Hans felt his heart gripped by an unbearable pain.
Remembering the flower he had promised to give the
Archbishop, he bent down and felt about amongst the
moss and fallen leaves to try and find one. The snow was
cold under his hands. Icy fingers squeezed his heart and
he fell spreadeagled over the frozen ground. He was
dead. The lay brother wept. He realised that he had killed
the abbot by destroying the heavenly joy he had yearned
for so much.

They carried Hans back to Oved. As the monks prepared
his body for burial, they found two shrivelled roots
tightly clasped in his right hand. The lay brother
hurriedly buried them in the garden, where he tended
them throughout the summer. That Christmas Eve,
the memory of the abbot weighed heavily on
him, and he went out into the garden that had
been so dear to Hans. There, where he had
planted the two shrivelled roots, glowed
beautiful flowers, their white petals glimmering

The Devil
personifies evil.
He was an
important feature
of Christianity in
the Middle Ages,
and was blamed
for all sorts of
illnesses and
disasters that
people had
no other way
of explaining.

From the early days of Christianity, hermits would cut themselves off from ordinary life, finding an isolated place in which they could give themselves up to a life of prayer. In the 3rd century, Saint Anthony went to live in the desert. His example was followed by many others.

in the dark. He called the monks, and showed them the heavenly flowers that had come from the Christmas forest of Göinge. The lay brother plucked one of the flowers and took it to the Archbishop. "Here is the gift abbot Hans promised you." The Archbishop went pale, and stood for a moment in silence. "Hans has kept his promise, now I will keep mine." And he gave the lay brother a letter of absolution to take to the robber.

It was Christmas Day as the lay brother climbed up to the robber's cave. "I'll kill you, you filthy monk," yelled the robber, "It's your fault that the forest will not come back in its Christmas beauty."

"It is indeed my fault, and mine alone," replied the lay brother, "and I'll gladly die for my sins, but before you kill me, read this letter." He gave the robber the letter of absolution. While the robber hesitated, his wife said firmly, "The abbot kept his word. Nevermore will the robber harm a living soul."

The robber and his family left the cave. The lay brother spent the rest of his life there, praying. But the forest never bloomed again. All that remains of that magical time is the Christmas rose.

The infant Jesus was lying asleep, when an old woman crept in.

From a French story by Jean and Jerome Tharaud.

The last visitor

It was dawn in Bethlehem. The stars were fading from the sky, the last of the pilgrims had left the stable, Mary had plumped up the straw, and at last the baby could sleep. But does anyone really sleep on Christmas night?

Softly the door swung open, more as if blown by a gust of wind than as if pushed by a hand, and a woman stood in the doorway. She was dressed in rags, and she was so old and brown and wrinkled, that her mouth looked like just another wrinkle across her aged face.

Seeing her, Mary grew afraid, as if some wicked fairy

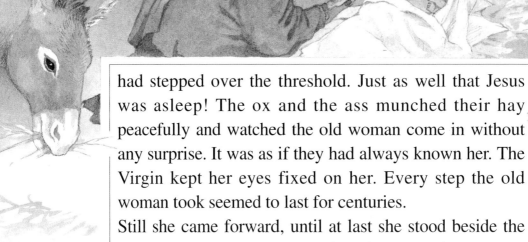

had stepped over the threshold. Just as well that Jesus was asleep! The ox and the ass munched their hay peacefully and watched the old woman come in without any surprise. It was as if they had always known her. The Virgin kept her eyes fixed on her. Every step the old woman took seemed to last for centuries.

Still she came forward, until at last she stood beside the crib. Thank God, Jesus was still asleep. But does anyone really sleep on Christmas night? All at once, he opened his eyes, and his mother was astonished to see that the woman's eyes and the eyes of the tiny baby were exactly the same and each gleamed with the same hope.

Then the old woman leant on the straw and fumbled in her rags, looking for something it seemed to take her an age to find. Mary watched her anxiously. The animals watched too, at peace, as if they had always known that she would come.

Finally, after what seemed an eternity, the old woman drew something out from her tattered clothes. Holding it hidden in her hand, she offered it to the baby.

After all the treasures brought by the kings and the gifts from the shepherds, what could this be? From where she sat, Mary could not see what it was. All that she could see was the old woman's back, bent with age, as she leant

The apple is important in many myths and legends. According to the ancient Greeks, it was the apple of discord which Paris gave to the goddess Aphrodite when he judged her to be the most beautiful goddess of all. But the golden apples of the gardens of the Hesperides brought immortality. For the Celts, apples were symbols of science, magic and divine revelation.

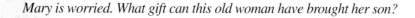

Mary is worried. What gift can this old woman have brought her son?

over the crib. But the ox and the ass could see, and still they were not surprised.

The scene seemed frozen in time, then gradually the old woman stood up, as if she had shed a heavy burden which had been weighing her down. Her shoulders were no longer bowed, her head nearly touched the ceiling, and her face had miraculously regained its youthful beauty. As the old woman moved away from the crib to leave the stable and disappear into the night, Mary at last saw the mysterious gift.

Eve, for it had been she, had given the baby a tiny apple, the apple of the first sin, the origin of so many others which followed. The tiny apple glowed red and round, held safely in the baby's hands, like a world newborn.

It was the custom in Paris, on Christmas Eve, not to eat apples, in memory of the first sin committed by Adam and Eve when they ate the forbidden fruit.

For Christians, Jesus brought redemption from sin. Below, Adam and Eve are sent out of Paradise.

Where do Christmas stories come from?

The unofficial gospels

The first stories about the birth of Jesus come from the gospels. There are other stories about Jesus' birth in the apocryphal gospels. The oldest and the best known of these dates from the second century and comes from Egypt or from Asia Minor. It is called the Proto-Gospel of Saint James. In this, there appear for the first time creatures such as the ox and the ass, never mentioned in the original gospels. Other, more magical, things occur too, especially during the flight into Egypt: leopards and lions worship the infant Christ, palm trees bow down to offer their fruit to Mary. All these elements built up into the colourful stories which formed the inspiration for paintings of the nativity and for carols.

Christmas stories

Christmas stories as we know them today only really began to be written in the 19th century. They are not only about the birth of Jesus, but about the miracle of hope, of a better world where the wicked stop behaving badly, where all children have loving homes, and where generosity and love overcome evil. They often incorporate local legends and beliefs and superstitions, some of which may be very old indeed. The greatest writer of Christmas stories was the English author Charles Dickens.

Christmas carols

The first Christmas songs were part of church services. Gradually, though, the story of the birth of Jesus, of the wise men and the shepherds was set to popular tunes of the day. In the 19th century, Christmas carols, printed on broadsheets, were sold in the streets by song-sellers. Soon some of the most famous poets, like Christina Rossetti, were writing Christmas carols which are still sung to this day.

The longest night

When was Jesus born? There are no full records of births from that time, but it was probably in 4 BC. In the 6th century, it was decided to record time as before or after the birth of Christ, but they were out in their calculations by about 4 years. Below, a Russian icon of the Nativity.

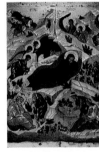

In the Middle Ages, All Fools Day carried on the tradition of the Saturnalia.

One date that nobody forgets is the 25th of December, Christmas Day. But Christmas was not always celebrated in December. The birth of Christ has been celebrated on the 6th of January, the 25th of March, the 10th of April and the 9th of May. It was only in the 14th century that the Church settled on the 25th of December. Before that, the most important celebrations always surrounded the resurrection of Jesus, on Easter Day.

Why the 25th of December?
From the beginning of time, the winter solstice, the longest night of the year, had been a time of festival and pagan rituals to ensure the return of the sun, the fertility of crops and the beginning of the new year. Christmas, which marks for Christians the birth of Christ and the beginning of a new world, was linked to the winter solstice and placed in December. It was also a way of wooing people away from the pagan rituals which still continued.

Saturnalia
In the Roman Empire, the festival of Saturnalia, which was held between the 17th and 24th of October, paid homage to Saturn, god of agriculture and crops, who was supposed to have reigned over a golden age in mythic times, an age in which everything was shared together and there were no slaves. During the Saturnalia, the usual social order was reversed: the slaves were waited on by their masters. All the usual social rules were suspended; it was a time of wild indulgence. It is likely that the festival once involved human sacrifice, as well as religious songs and dances.
After the Saturnalia, in the Roman calendar, there came the Calends, the

Centre, top: the God Saturn according to a 15th-century fresco.

A 10th-century statue of Freya German goddess of fertility.

Christmas com from Old Engl meaning Chris Mass. Yule is another Old English word, brought over b invaders from North. Noël, th French for Christmas, eith comes from th Latin natalis, meaning birth, or from the Ol French noio, which means r sun, linking it one of the man origins of this festival. The German Weinachten means holy nig

New Year, when friends would visit each other, partying together and exchanging gifts: leafy branches, candles and reed dolls in memory of the children who had once been sacrificed to the Phoenician god Baal, who was associated with the Roman god Saturn and the Greek god Chronos. There was also a festival especially for children, the Dies Juvenalis.

In northern lands

The winter solstice was celebrated at Yuletide (in Sweden, Father Christmas is called Jultomte). Traces of these old festivals can still be found in the Christmas customs of today. The Yuletide celebrations were held in honour of some of the most important gods in nordic mythology. A first toast was drunk to Odin, god of War and of Poetry, to honour his position as god of the Dead. Second and third toasts were drunk to Njord and Freja, goddesses of fertility and plenty.

In some areas, it was thought that the god Wotan (the German name for Odin) rode from house to house, carrying presents and bringing a burning log.

Once a year, the Goths had a day of communal charity. The poorest people in the village laid a pine branch or a bundle of straw on their doorstep, while the richer villagers collected gifts from each other in the name of Wotan, and then distributed them to the poor, going round the village at night in a torchlit procession. The whole community would then gather around a tree which had been brought into the centre of the village. Torches were stuck in the ground at the four points of the compass, and a sacrifice was made to Wotan – an oxen decorated with flowers, or, sometimes, a prisoner of war. Then the tree was set alight, and people would sing and dance and drink around the blazing fire.

All these festivals were dedicated to death and rebirth. This time, when the old order was finished and the new year was about to begin, was the time chosen for Christmas. For Christians, a new world is born through Jesus, when God became man, died and rose again, so that all humanity might live with God for ever more.

The festival of death and rebirth, after an engraving by F. Barth.

The Persian cult of Mithras was introduced to Rome in 218 AD. Mithras was a sun god whose birth was celebrated on the 25th of December. He was worshipped in tiny underground temples. Below, Mithras is seen sacrificing a bull, a symbol of life.

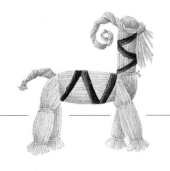

Rites and rituals

Advent

Christmas Eve is the last day of four weeks of spiritual preparation, a period of waiting called Advent In the Middle Ages, it was a time of fasting when people did not eat meat. As Christmas approached, signs of celebration began to appear. Decorations would go up in the houses and carol singers would sing in the streets.

Nowadays, children are given Advent calendars, with 25 little windows marking the 25 days of December to Christmas. A new window is opened each day, with the final window showing the nativity. In Scandinavia, families get out their advent candlestick, which has four candleholders. On the first Sunday of December, one candle is lit and then put out. On the second Sunday, two candles are lit, and so on, until, on Christmas Day, all four candles are lit and kept burning brightly throughout the

celebrations. In Germany, there is a similar ritual involving the Christmas crown, a circle of twisted branches decorated with ribbons and candles which is hung up at the beginning of Advent.

Christmas Eve

It is a common tradition to clean the house from cellar to attic in preparation for Christmas. In Ireland, everything is washed, even the buildings themselves! In Norway, the last Sunday in Advent is called Dirty Sunday – by the end of the day every ornament in the house is sparkling clean!

A Polish Tree of Life, made of bread. There are all sorts of different kinds of Christmas cakes and biscuits made all over Europe: gingerbread pigs in Germany, gingerbread and cinnamon houses in Denmark.

In northern Europe and North America, a Christmas crown is decorated with candles and hung from the ceiling or placed on a table. Sometimes it is hung on the front door as a Christmas wreath, to mark the festival.

Top of page: a straw ram, a memory of the old pagan festival which marked the winter solstice

Below, a crib from Provence, in France.

Before Midnight s, the Christmas was lit in front of the family. All the lights in the house were put out, the fire was doused, and the log was lit, ng a fresh spark r a flame which ad been fetched om the Church. hen the log was sprinkled with ly water, wine, milk or honey. wadays, the log survives as a chocolate cake.

In the last century, in Sweden and Finland, people would clean themselves thoroughly in a sauna, and then put on clean clothes, and sometimes new ones, before joining friends and family for Christmas.

In different countries, Christmas begins at different times – in Poland it starts when the first star appears, in Brittany at the ninth star (in memory of the nine months of Mary's pregnancy, in Finland when the bells have rung out from Turku Cathedral...

In Catholic and Protestant countries alike, Christmas Eve is often spent playing games together or in spiritual preparation for midnight service. Then, that night or the next day, there is the big family meal, or Christmas dinner. Wherever Christmas is celebrated, there will be at least one of the symbols of Christmas: a crib, a tree or a log, thus recalling fertility rites, fire festivals, and the renewal of Nature as well as the birth of Christ.

The Christmas log

This began as a branch from a fruit tree, or from a forest tree such as an oak or beech, which was brought into the house in the hope that the New Year would bring in a good harvest. In Burgundy and Catalonia, presents are laid along the log.

The Christmas tree

The use of greenery in winter festivals goes back to the earliest times. During the Saturnalia, the Romans decorated their houses with leaves and branches. In northern lands, Yule was celebrated by torchlight around a forest tree. In the miracle plays which were acted out in churches in the Middle Ages, a fir tree, an evergreen, was brought into church to symbolise the tree of the knowledge of good and evil which stood in the garden of Eden. When miracle plays were suppressed, the faithful would bring a fir tree into their houses on the 24th December, the festival of Adam and Eve.

The crib

From the earliest days of Christianity, the grotto in Bethlehem where Jesus was supposed to have been born was a place of pilgrimage. In the 4th century, small chapels modelled on the grotto were built in churches. Figures of the Virgin and Child were placed inside. Soon, models of the grotto, the crib and the holy family were made for the home, as they are today.

In 1223, St Francis of Assisi said: "I wish to do something which will recall the little child who was born in Bethlehem and set before our eyes in some way his poverty and his infant needs." Below, a Nativity Scene by Giotto (14th century).

Christmas trees began in a small way in the 15th century. In the 19th century they became a traditional part of Christmas the world over.

Christmas presents

Below, Saint Nicholas dips naughty children, who had been unkind to Africans, into a huge inkwell to turn them black.

This wicked goblin, with his vicious whip, terrified children for centuries.

Deep in the night on Christmas Eve is the magical time when Father Christmas creeps from house to house, bringing presents to lay under the tree, in stockings or pillow-cases, in clogs before the fire-place or at the foot of the bed.

There was not always a link between the birth of Jesus and presents for children, nor was it always Father Christmas who brought them. Traditional figures such as Saint Martin, Saint Catherine and Saint Andrew swept through the skies and into the houses, on feast days between the 11th of November and the 6th of January. Nowadays, there is only Father Christmas.

Saint Nicholas

His feast day is on the 5th of December, and on the night between the 5th and 6th he travels from house to house in the Czech Republic, in Holland and in Germany together with his servant, Black Peter, rewarding good children and punishing those who have behaved badly.

For children in Holland, he comes on a boat from Spain, dressed as a bishop, while Black Peter's face is smeared with soot. Riding a beautiful white horse, he is at the head of a procession into the centre of Amsterdam to meet the mayor or even the Queen. He may also go into the schools and read the school records to see which children have been good and which bad, giving presents to the good children while Black Peter beats the bad ones with a broom. Then, overnight, he rides on his white horse over the rooftops, leaving presents on the hearth or in a basket placed by the door, where the children have left some hay and carrots for his horse.

The night of December 24th

There are all sorts of people who were supposed to travel the skies or to come out of the earth. In Sweden, the Jultomte was originally a skinny goblin who was given offerings by the peasants so that he would not bring them bad luck and in turn gave presents to the children. In Germany, Frau Holle might bring presents, or she might play nasty practical jokes. In the

Nicholas was a bishop who lived in Asia Minor in the 4th century. He is supposed to have performed all sorts of miracles: he rescued sailors from drowning (see the picture at the top of the page, taken from a 15th century Hungarian painting), and brought to life some children who had been killed and put in barrels of brine by a wicked butcher.

The Dutch name for Saint Nicholas is Santa Claus, and this is the name by which Father Christmas is often known in England and in the United States.

La Befana has something of the witch about her. She flies through the sky on a broomstick, looking for the Infant Jesus. Saint Nicholas sent her away but Saint Joseph explained to her that the Infant Jesus exists in every child. Since then, in Italy, it is she who brings presents to the children.

Spain, the three wise men give out presents. They march at the head of a splendid procession. Children leave their shoes out on the balconies for them. Sometimes the shoes are stuffed with hay, so that the wise men's camels can have something to eat.

Franche-Comté, in France, it was Tante Arié who came visiting. She is pictured as having a beautiful face, but with teeth made of steel and the webbed feet of a goose. She wore a crown and carried a bell which announced her arrival as she travelled through the region, bringing presents for the children and, sometimes, throwing naughty children into the river.

These figures, part goblin and part fairy, have all given way to the Christkindl and to Father Christmas.

Christkindl, or the Christ Child

In Switzerland and in Alsace, children are told that it is the Christ Child who brings them their presents. In Alsace, though, he appears as a young girl dressed in white, a crown on her head and carrying a sceptre with a star on its tip. She is followed by a dark figure with a long white beard, who carries a sack on his back, bulging with all sorts of presents, with a whip sticking out of the top. The children recite poems and receive gifts – or a whipping.

Father Christmas

Father Christmas is the most widespread bringer of presents nowadays. He seems to be a mixture of all sorts of different figures from Germany, the Netherlands, Alsace and elsewhere. When people from Europe emigrated to America, they took their stories with them. Over time, the stories were mixed together and out of

these came Father Christmas. Saint Nicholas moved his visits from early December to Christmas Eve, his horse became a sledge drawn by eight reindeer, and Black Peter disappeared.

The fat, cheerful figure of Father Christmas with his flowing white beard and his red robes trimmed with white fur is a universal Christmas figure the world over. From Switzerland to South Africa, from Portugal to Peru, he flies ever further, bringing gifts to the children of the world.

Epiphany, the 6th of January

Epiphany, or Twelfth Night, is the day when Christians in the West celebrate the visit of the wise men to baby Jesus. It marks the end of Christmas. In some countries, it is at Epiphany that presents are given out. In Bavaria, it is Berchta who brings them, in Italy, la Befana, and in Spain, the three wise men. Berchta used to be a witch who travelled with Wotan at the head of the procession of the dead, but once a year, her face covered by a horned mask, she gave out presents or punishments.

In Russia, it was Jack Frost who gave out the presents on Saint Sylvester's Day.

The Christmas fairy, followed by Hans Trapp, who punished naughty children.

Look out for other titles in this series:

SARAH, WHO LOVED LAUGHING
A TALE FROM THE BIBLE

THE SECRETS OF KAIDARA
AN ANIMIST TALE FROM AFRICA

I WANT TO TALK TO GOD
A TALE FROM ISLAM

THE RIVER GODDESS
A TALE FROM HINDUISM

CHILDREN OF THE MOON
YANOMAMI LEGENDS

I'LL TELL YOU A STORY
TALES FROM JUDAISM

THE PRINCE WHO BECAME A BEGGAR
A BUDDHIST TALE

JESUS SAT DOWN AND SAID...
THE PARABLES OF JESUS

SAINT FRANCIS, THE MAN WHO SPOKE TO BIRDS
TALES OF ST FRANCIS OF ASSISI

MUHAMMAD'S NIGHT JOURNEY
A TALE FROM ISLAM